Zulu Poems

Mazisi Kunene

Zulu Poems

AFRICANA PUBLISHING CORPORATION
NEW YORK

Published
in the United States of America 1970
by Africana Publishing Corporation
101 Fifth Avenue
New York, N.Y. 10003

Library of Congress catalog card no. 70-136492
ISBN 0-8419-0061-2

Printed in Great Britain

Contents

Introduction

The poems contained in this volume are taken from several volumes of poems I originally wrote in Zulu. I selected them on the basis of their translatability and the variety of types they represent. I omitted poems wherever I felt that they failed in translation to convey adequately the ideas contained in the original. I do not claim here to have overcome the age-old problems of translation, problems which I found even more complex since I had to translate from a language with a different structure and a completely different cultural history and background. These will be dealt with in greater detail in the latter part of this introduction. But before discussing them, let me give the general background from which the poems evolve.

Zulu literature, of which this collection is part, has a long history of development. Yet it remains largely unknown for two important reasons. Firstly, it is an oral literature (at least until it was recorded recently), and as such largely depends for its survival on special institutions devised to preserve it. Some of these are associated with the traditional ancestral religion, which, by its very nature, demands reverence towards the oral statements made by ancestors whose deeds the poems recorded. Other institutions arose directly out of the need to propagate the communal ethic, as for instance, the common evening story-telling. And to preserve this oral literature, a large number of literary competitions and festivals were held. Outstanding poets and story-tellers were regarded so highly that the community saw to their maintenance. This enabled them to move freely from area to area reciting to highly enthusiastic and critical audiences. Through such institutions and various other mnemonic devices, Zulu society was able to preserve its literature almost intact through many generations.

Colonisation is the next important factor to obscure this literature. The conquest of the African people led to frantic attempts by both missionaries and administrators to eliminate traditional values, except where they furthered the interests of the conquerors. Inevitably this led to the destruction of the very institutions which had acted as a creative force. The reasons and motives for this differed but the results were the same. The administrator wanted to use the black population as a cheap labour reservoir. To achieve this, he systematically drove it away from the land, which had formed the very basis of its culture. In doing so, he dispersed the population, substituting an individualistic money economy for a highly communal social organisation. And to promote trade among the 'natives', the administrator continuously preached the superiority of his way of life. Through western books, with their highly biased accounts of history, he blocked any possibilities of self-discovery. A people grew up whose whole ethos was of foreign derivation, who not only aspired to the things of 'the white man' but also looked at its own history with revulsion.

The missionary performed an equally zealous task. He preached about a god, whose repugnance for the ways of the pagans proved to be based on English cultural criteria. Indeed, his disapproval in most cases closely matched the interests of the British Empire; thus the black Christians fought zealously against those whom they were taught were pagans and antichrists. As their material standards improved through such incentives as the vote for the wealthy and the 'educated', they not only completely rejected their culture but developed a *tabula rasa* mentality into which nothing 'native' intruded, unless strictly approved by the missionaries. They totally embraced the ideology of individualism, and thus became known amongst non-Christians as the 'stingy ones', or 'they who cook in a small pot'.

Since generosity and the concept of sharing constituted the very basis of traditional philosophy, these acts and attitudes indicated how deeply the black converts had been alienated from their culture.

What happened in the missionary schools was even more tragic in so far as African traditional literature and culture was concerned. The missionary and the administrator combined efforts to promulgate rules by which African language and traditional cultural expressions (such as dancing, 'excited participation' and 'body exposure') were forbidden at the risk of incurring serious punishment such as hard labour and ridicule. On the other hand, English language, English country dances, and English styles of clothing were yoked round the necks of the pupils. Of course, 'excited participation' and 'body exposure' were all matters of cultural definition. The effect was to deprive African literature of some of its components, precisely because African literature required communal participation, and, for its expression, body movements in their minutest forms. And the vast ignorance and usual arrogance of conquerors also meant that in defining African literature and philosophies they relegated them to the lowest level of expression.

These few poems will have served their purpose if they stimulate some understanding of the true nature of African thought and literature. What is traditional African literature? What are its origins? How does it differ from other literatures? These are some of the questions to be dealt with.

Zulu literature, like most African literatures, is communal. This has fundamental stylistic and philosophical implications. The communal organisation in Africa is not just a matter of individuals clinging together to eke out an existence, as some have claimed, nor is it comparable (except very superficially) to the rural communities in Europe. It is a communal organisation which has evolved its own ethic, its own philosophical system, its own forms of projecting and interpreting its realities and experiences. Nor does it relate its evolution to an urban centre. In brief, it is a communal structure which has affirmed its particularity through forms of religion and thought arising directly out of its organisation. It believes, for instance, that the highest virtue is not justice (perhaps one should mention that justice is the expression of an individualised society which finds thereby a means of minimising its inevitable frictions), but heroism, that is, self-sacrifice on behalf of the community. Accordingly, it has developed a highly sophisticated heroic epic. Where individualistic societies read 'I', this philosophy requires one to read 'I on behalf of'. Thus when a Zulu greets, he says (even if he is alone) '*sawubona*' meaning 'we see you', or more accurately, 'I on behalf of my family or community pay our respects to you.' He may even say '*sanibona*' meaning 'I on behalf of my family pay our respects to you and your family.'

All these facts are relevant to understanding a literature which has evolved in a communal context. The literature, to have meaning for the community, uses a kind of shorthand system, comprising communally evolved symbols which represent a special system of ideas.

In this sense symbols, at least some of them, have specific cultural meanings. In order to understand fully the poetry or literature, the cultural significance of the symbols themselves must be understood. Many ignorant foreigners, for instance, have remarked on what they call savage or barbaric grunts, or else utterances which they call meaningless sounds. To an African these 'grunts' and utterances have appropriate symbolic significance and elicit appropriate emotional responses.

Zulu poetry being communal, requires a special method of presentation. The poet does not just recite his poetry but acts it, uses variations of pitch, and aims at communicating his poem through the stimulation of all the senses. He produces at one level a symphonic chant, at another, a drama, and still another, a dance. The audience is thus held spellbound, not only by the meaning of words and their sounds but also by the performance. The audience demonstrates its approval or participation by either imitating the poet's movements or devising appropriate actions related to the meanings of the words. This is accompanied by cries of '*musho!*' meaning 'praise him' (the hero).

Almost every member of society has his 'praise-poem' which is either given to him or made by himself about his deeds. If he makes a praise-poem about himself, this is not self-praise in the individualistic sense, but an appeal for social approval for the contributions made to society.

It is on the basis of things done, and on the basis of an awareness of obligations expected by the community that the individual composes his poem; thus his 'praise' is an affirmation of a social ethic. Many who do not understand African communal ideology condemn its literature for what they consider to be vainglorious statements; yet the poets did not only praise socially approved acts, but condemned socially repugnant ones as well. The word 'bonga' (to praise) itself is exchangeable with the word condemn. The great nineteenth-century poet Mshongweni says of Dingane, the king of the Zulus:

You coward who deserted your own armies.

In another part of his heroic epic he condemns the king for having killed his own brothers to gain power:

Your heart is black,
You killed Mhlangana, the son of your father.

Of Mpande, king of the Zulus, the poet says:

You are a ruler who rules over women,

a great insult to any Zulu bred in the military ethic and trained to think of women as incapable of brave actions.

The best south African poetry is epitomised by the heroic epic. The Zulu heroic epic has gone through different states of development, from about the early seventeenth century up to the present day. Since African literature expresses the historical state of the community, the poet does not speculate in the abstract or indulge in his individualistic fantasies. He is a recorder of events, an evaluator of his era in relation to other eras. He has to know in detail the historically significant occasions, select from them the most symbolically representative and on that evolve or affirm an ethic. Because of this closeness of literature to history, the literature follows peaks and troughs according to the historical periods. Thus Ndaba (a seventeenth-century ruler of the Zulus) is depicted only as a hunter with a shield on his knees. The period from the sixteenth century to about 1815 abounds in poetry obsessed with physical appearance as an aesthetic quality. It is also characterised by frequent occurrence of erotic metaphor. From this we can deduce that the community was less active compared to the later epic exploits that were to characterise it. Needless to say, the earlier poetry lacks the depth and the colourful imagery of other later periods.

The upheavals caused by land hunger in the period about 1795–1815 resulted in the creation of the Zulu empire through the military genius of Shaka. In creating an empire, Shaka stimulated the greatest period of Zulu traditional literature.

Magolwane, Shaka's court poet, revolutionised Zulu poetry and created not only a form that was the highest vehicle of thought and feeling, but also evolved such a dramatic style of language that legend has it he needed only to beat the ground with his staff to emphasise the meaning of his poem. This in itself meant that personal performance had been superseded by the importance of words. Of course, Magolwane was part of a tradition, but his genius gave it its fullest expression. The symbols he chose were not only aimed at showing parallel qualities but also the fusion of related qualities. In his epic, he combined both analysis and synthesis so that his stanzas not only introduced and treated the subject, but also contained philosophical conclusions and summaries.

It is not possible in this introduction to give a detailed account of Magolwane's varied contributions to Zulu poetry. He created a dramatic epic for which he evolved a complex form. For instance, when Magolwane depicts a dramatically powerful situation, he uses lowering consonants and, similarly, when he expresses feelings of tenderness he uses nasals, and sibilants, together with other softer consonants:

Usidlukula – dlwedlwe
Siyadla sidlondlobele
Sibeke izihlangu emadolweni
(Wild one who towers as he
eats with shields on his knees)

Here he depicts the dramatic urgency with which Shaka eats
shortly before joining battle. There can be no accurate translation
in English since so much meaning is conveyed through sounds.
Magolwane was succeeded by Mshongweni, another great
poet who is philosophical, detached, with an acid tongue. He
portrays a growing cynicism in the period of the less able King
Dingane, who followed Shaka as the ruler of the Zulus. Of Din-
gane, Mshongweni says:

You the variegated butterfly of Phunga and Mageba
Which when I touched so lightly, it frowned.

With the disintegration of the Zulu empire, poetry suffered
equally but retained some of its vitality and quality. This latter
period is characterised by a nostalgic feeling for former military
power.

Other African peoples of southern Africa show equal merit in
their poetry according to the period of their history and national
expression. For instance, Xhosa poetry has a rich tradition which
was revived in more recent times by the great Xhosa poet,
Mqhayi. The same can be said for Sotho poetry. The glorification
of Zulu poetry as something unique should be avoided.

There are other interesting forms of poetry which have not so
far been mentioned. Among them is the satirical poem, the form
of which arises out of the communal structure and the oral nature
of the poetry. The satirical poem is highly rhythmical. Basically
it aims at exciting the rhythmic sense in children, who become the
vehicles and popularisers of social criticism; though of course
they are not always aware of its meaning. Such poems deal with

15

anti-social behaviour and are generally designed in question and answer form. Usually one individual states and develops the theme while the others egg him on with provocative statements until the poem reaches an ethical conclusion:

> On vanity
> ALL: Woman who lives across the stream
> What is it that you boast about?
> ONE: I boast about my new skirt
> ALL: What skirt do you boast about?
> ONE: It is a beautiful soft garment
> ALL: Softness is also of the brain.
> The fall of a big tree crashes and
> Whimpers on the ground like a dog.

These dramatised forms may of course be used to popularise non-satirical themes but more often than not they aim to make a critical point.

Other forms of poetry derive from the epic (e.g. poems in praise of bulls, birds, etc.):

> O my bull, they have touched you in your sleep,
> You woke up and threw the earth into darkness.

In this type the improviser is making a factual point which may be either taken literally or symbolically, as meaning those who provoke war. One of the main characteristics of Zulu poetry is its concrete imagery: it derives from every day experience, it is natural that its language and symbols should be concrete. It is important always to bear this in mind, as most statements which may appear didactic in translation or appear to contain spiritual implications, are in fact far from having such connotations. When someone says in Zulu or Xhosa 'I hope we shall meet again', he is not expressing a spiritual desire, but means simply that 'your actions and my actions should be such that we meet again; if you fail or I do, the responsibility is ours.' This idea is sometimes carried so far that when mourning a dead friend, the poet chastises him for having let him down, for having allowed death to take him when they should have met. People have been heard to say: 'Don't you dare die before I see you.'

Again, according to the Zulu cultural tradition, the moon, the sun, and the stars are physical phenomena which primarily express the nature of distance and the quality of light, while also being symbolic of (physical) power. All this does not mean that Zulu poetry is without fantasy, yet such fantasies are firmly rooted in actual experiences. Abstract ideas are projected through the use of concrete images. Love is not love as an idea, but as the outcome of social actions and considerations by two individuals in direct relation to the requirements of their social groups.

Since the African translates external realities into terms of his immediate relations within his social group, he does not generally consider the world outside his immediate experience to be composed of hostile (abstract or mythological) forces. Beyond the known, there are always people who, though different or even contemptible, are basically the same. His conception of mankind is therefore of a number of people who have the same faults, defects or merits as his everyday experience dictates, rather than the spiritualised or ideological mankind, with its moralistic connotations, which is evoked in European cultures.

The concept of the 'other world of ancestral spirits' is equally concrete. It is a place of rest peopled with former relatives who retain the same qualities as they had when alive. They are generous or acid-tempered according to what they were before their death. Cultures with elaborate fantasies about the afterlife may well see this conception as simple, but the Zulu would see the fantasising in those cultures as itself childish and unrealistic.

It is important to note that, before the coming of Christianity, 'sin' was not an act committed against a supernatural force but directly against society, and it was punishable by society – unless of course such an act threatened the complete annihilation of society. The moral evaluations are therefore different here. In the same way cosmological concepts derived equally from observation and everyday experience. The world was conceived as round with four points of the compass (*umhlaba omagumbe mane*). The stars were sources of light which most probably were giving light to other worlds peopled by other people. There could be no infinity as an abstraction, but a series of concrete existences stretching to no end. Thus, furthest away was the 'place of dogs', which was in turn beyond 'the place of the mother of the sun'. The symbol of this unity was the circle. The concept of the circle contained in it the idea of the family, of time division, of periods of existence, of the very shape and form of the universe. Even the circular structure of his house emphasised this philosophy. The circle was not therefore a mathematical abstract but a physical reality with the associations of everyday reality.

There is also another concept which must be borne in mind in understanding the meanings of African or Zulu poetry. Things are what they are by virtue of their own qualities and also by virtue of the values we place on them. Their qualities may release forces which are inimical to us, but that does not mean that they themselves are destructive. The neutral characteristics of the thing in itself and our evaluative system are not contradictory but complementary. There is no morality attached to the action of 'opposing forces'; they are neither evil nor good, and when we describe them as evil we are in fact not describing them, but how they impinge on us or on their opposites. This dualism means that there are two levels of action or meaning possible, both equally valid in their own terms. The first level may symbolise through its qualities the meanings of the second level i.e. our meanings. The result of this is that there is no sentimentalising about things since they cannot act as substitutes for human realities, but only as their symbols in a very direct sense. A flower, in traditional Zulu literature, is not beautiful *per se*, but contains qualities of beauty which can only be realisable (since the flower itself is unaware of its appearance, beauty being an attribute accorded by us) if paralleled with similar qualities to those we perceive in man. Because of these reasons, and because of its communal origins, African poetry is highly centred on man and man's actions in society. The double levels of meaning have given rise to many interesting devices of form, types of insinuation and linkings, which we cannot go into here.

This introduction deals briefly with aspects of Zulu poetry which, I hope, the reader will bear in mind in attempting to understand this collection of poems. These are not English poems but poems directly evolved from a Zulu literary tradition.

Modern Zulu poets like Vilakazi, Mthembu, Made, S. Dlamini, A. Kunene, when first attempting to put in writing what had been an oral tradition, faced immeasurable problems. First, because they had been brought up on a tradition of English poetry they found themselves confined to English literary forms and styles. This assumed such bizarre proportions that, for instance, though the Zulu language structure does not lend itself to rhymes, words were twisted to express this form. Some of the poems are hardly intelligible, because of their preoccupation with form. The second problem they faced was psychological one. Since Zulu traditional poetry had expressed themes connected with actions of the community, they found it difficult to find new themes other than those dictated by English poetry. The result was that though culturally the African does not indulge in effusions about natural beauty (because of his philosophical approach and anthropocentric conceptions of life), the new poets plunged themselves into ecstatic descriptions of natural beauties. As this experience was secondary (being derived from contact with a foreign culture) it expressed itself in imitative terms. Most of the new Zulu poetry became an imitation of, in particular, nineteenth-century English poets like Keats, Shelley and Wordsworth. Predominant themes tended to centre round religion (e.g. Mthembu and Made), death (as a point of final annihilation and loss) and nostalgia about past history (not as an assertion of the self but as an act of despair). The selection of themes was indicative of the hollow despair which these new poets felt.

As the Zulu literary tradition had been devalued, I started writing without models, until I discovered Vilakazi's poetry. When I became dissatisfied with Vilakazi and others, I started my own metrical experiments based on the recurrence of stress in the penultimate syllable. Finding this unsatisfactory, I then experimented with syllabic metre, but eventually discarded all these experiments in preference for an internal rhythm which I found in studying traditional poetry. This is the method I have found most appropriate to Zulu poetry.

In conclusion, I should mention that these poems could not have been translated without the insistence and assistance of Gillian Frost, who, in helping with the translation, discussed the themes and ideas of the originals, and thus helped to keep their spirit and meanings intact.

Notes on the Poems

Poems in this volume incorporate cultural influences which are reshaped and modified to fit in with Zulu traditional literary concepts; for instance, though the elegy does not exist in Zulu, a new type has been evolved, expressing Zulu elegiac feelings in a framework derived from those cultures that have this form.

Proper names in Zulu poetry are sometimes used as a literary device. In such cases they do not necessarily refer to a real person, but are part of a system of ideas or personifications. This is only possible because proper names are more than labels but bear meanings expressive of events (e.g. Sompiyezwe: father of the world war, that is, born during the world war), of desires (e.g. Nokuthula: mother of peace), of celebrated occasions (e.g. Bafabegiya: they died singing). For example:

> May I when I awake
> Take from all men
> The yearnings of their souls
> And turn them into the fountain of Mpindelela
> Which will explode into oceans;
> Not those of the south that are full of bitterness
> But those that are sweet to taste.

Here we can assume firstly that there is such a fountain (ideally there ought to be) or secondly, that the name Mpindelela – 'recurrent' – is descriptive of recurrent yearnings, or thirdly, that the name describes the action of the fountain. The apparent meaning, namely a desire to drink and rest with others at the fountain of Mpindelela, must be as intense and satisfying as if this was the only meaning possible in the poem. On the other hand, if we have understood the poem in its metaphorical sense, the concept of the fountain is extended in its meaning by the name Mpindelela. The dual levels of meaning often interact, share the verbal meanings and implications. This interplay between the two levels of meaning can be observed in poems like 'Thoughts on a Gathering Storm', 'Your Footprints' (referring either to an individual or a tyrannical regime), 'Invocation to Life', and 'Valley of Rest'.

NOTE III

Some concepts have particular significance which may only be fully understood within the values attached to them by the Zulu cultural experience.

The Shade: The importance of the shade in a hot environment can be fully understood by the number of myths to which it has given rise. The shade is more than a place where one can shelter from the sun; it is a place where important gatherings were held, where travellers could find refuge and where thinkers could meditate. Similar factors operate in the case of rivers and fountains.

The Sun: Because of its overpowering heat, its dominating presence and its awe-inspiring distance the sun acquired special significance. Daily life was not divided into time units but into cycles. Using the sun as a point of reference, the day had seven cycles: early morning cycle (*uvivi, insakusa* or *ekuseni kokusa*), 5 a.m.–6.30 a.m. approximately; mid-morning cycle (*ekuseni*), 6.30 a.m.–10.30 a.m. approximately; early midday cycle (*ekuseni kwasemini*), 10.30 a.m.–12 noon approximately; midday cycle (*emini*), 12 noon–1.30 p.m. approximately; early afternoon cycle (*emini yantambama*), 1.30 p.m.–3 p.m. approximately; mid-afternoon cycle (*ntambama*), 3 p.m.–5 p.m. approximately; late afternoon cycle (*intambama yasebusuku*), literally meaning the afternoon of the night. Owing to the preparations and important changes necessary to adjust to the night, the late afternoon cycle acquired particular importance. Hence many myths were created associated with late afternoon cycles. For instance, the reference in these poems to the place of the setting sun or place of the sinking sun is mythical, referring (according to the context) to distant places, mythological regions, etc.

Travellers: Many romantic stories and myths are associated with travellers, who in old days were very common. The traveller acquired a special place in the culture both because many people were themselves likely to travel (*unyawo alunampumulo* – the feet know no rest) and also because the traveller put to test what was one of the most important ethical demands, namely, generosity. Unless you had been generous to a stranger whom you may never have met again, your generosity was still in doubt. This gave rise to a number of idioms like 'never shut your door to a stranger', 'no hill is without a graveyard' (a man can die among strangers who must bury him as if he was one of them).

Concept of period of life (e.g. ages of man, generations, thousand years): These concepts must be understood as actual periods of time. They refer immediately and specifically to realities of community life, and do not have the abstract features that they might have in English. 'Generations to come', for instance, refers to the generations to come, not only in religious but also in physical terms. The survival of this generation is an expression of the survival of the past generation.

Ancestral belief requires that each generation considers itself as part of a past generation to which it is obligated. This interdependence between generations is so strong that each generation is eager to assure the well-being of the next generation not only for the sake of that generation but for its own sake. In order to emphasise this, any living member expects his ancestors to perform certain duties, e.g. taking requests to God. If his ancestors fail to carry out these duties, he can 'starve' them or refuse them sacrifice. In this sense, generations become a series of inter-connected existences. Similarly a thousand years is a thousand years of existences realised in those who are part of that time span. Life, in short, is according to this philosophy an alteration of cycles of existence between generations. A generation might or might not make history – all the same, its life and reality is assured by the obligations owed to it by the next generation.

Heritage: In the context of this belief, one's inheritance not only is of importance in terms of its material aspects, but also represents the obligations that the past generation has conferred on members of the next. The heir is in this sense a trustee who is given the responsibility of dispersing his wealth with fairness and justice, and in so doing is morally obligated to his ancestors. No court of law could intervene in these matters. Heirs receive a special veneration even from their own fathers, who proudly mention them among other friends as *'indlafa yami'* (my heir).

Umbilical cord: The umbilical cord is regarded as a symbol em-phasising the unity between generations. After it has been removed, it is carefully buried. Thus, a Zulu will refer to his place of birth as 'the place where my umbilical cord is.' In short, the person considers himself part of the soil where his umbilical cord is buried, uniting him not only with the present generation of his family but also with the past.

Circular pot: In traditional drinking gatherings a circular pot is used. To symbolise communal unity individuals drink from the same pot. This was further emphasised by the strict rule of receiving and passing on the beer pot, even if one does not drink.

NOTE IV

The Elegy: In traditional Zulu poetry elegiac feelings were ex-pressed in understatements. The person either referred to death in general terms or swore revenge at whoever he thought had caused the death of his friend or relative. I have used this technique (the understatement) here in the poems 'Elegy to Galo', 'Elegy for Donda', 'On the death of the young guerillas'. The understatement produces its own horror by the sudden realisation it creates that however 'frivolous' the treatment of the subject, the loss is intense and real. In this way, the reader or listener is made to experience the feelings of loss in his own terms, the poem merely providing a reminder of the realities of life.

NOTE V

The satirical conversational form has been modified for use in types of poems other than is traditionally done, e.g. 'Elegy for Msizi', 'A great generation', 'Two wise men'. Here the form has been used in non-satirical types of poems.

NOTE VI

African resistance poems either mourn the loss of the country to foreigners (not in pathetic terms but as a technique) or describe them in deprecatory terms. This is the technique I have used in 'Your footprints', 'Europe', 'Political prisoner', 'Avenge'. From the days of early clashes with Europeans, African poets have set out to define tasks, explode myths of invincibility, reaffirm the values of their society. Cultural values are projected as being superior to those of the occupying forces. To elevate these values, Zulu poets sometimes went even to the extremes of praising the heroism of the enemy. But this itself showed a deep sense of confidence. Some examples of early resistance poetry:

Fight and return in time, son of Ndaba
Remember the white man bears bitter grudges

It is these white men my lord
Who have done strange things
They defecate in the house like a child

In short there is no tradition of poetry that elevates abstract
values such as liberty. Poetry of this type asserts concrete com-
munal values.

NOTE VII

The Epic: The epic does not aim at narrating mythologies of the
past but at projecting the conceptions of life and the universe
according to African (Zulu) belief and interpretation. I have used
the story of the origin of life and added my own detailed descrip-
tions according to the dictates of Zulu culture. There is no Sodume
in Zulu mythology but there is an undefined idea of the female
and male thunder which I chose to call Nodume and Sodume.
Nomkhubulwane, goddess of Plenty, does exist and so does the
concept of a universal creator. In order to build up a contradictory
but complementary system (as evolved by Zulu philosophies) I
have allied Nomkhubulwane with Sodume and Nodume pre-
cisely because thunder and fertility are associated concepts among
the Zulu people. I have not however presented Somazwi as the
devil since such a concept does not exist in traditional Zulu
thought. He is the opposing force which has good and valid
questions to put. The idea of triumph of good over evil does not
exist in Zulu mythology. That which has the greater force
triumphs, and must be paid the tribute it deserves, on its own
terms. That does not mean, however, that force is glorified;
it is only assumed that in order to triumph such a force must
contain in it a higher morality and will, which it will use
creatively. Thus when individual combatants fight, it is the duty
of the winner to clean the wounds of the defeated, to compensate,
if damage is excessive. As the epic develops there will be no

26

Satan banished into limbo and made to suffer eternal damnation. Such an action would damn the victor and show him as weak. The characters depicted here are not really gods, at least in the sense of Yoruba, Greek, and Roman gods, but personalised ideas. This may well be true of other gods, but the difference perhaps here is that whereas other gods represented an individualised external reality and therefore had more direct responsibilities to the life of the community or individuals, these 'gods' represent only personalised speculation. A Zulu may indeed (traditionally) think of the shrieking thunder-sound as representing the female and the more powerful thunder-sound as representing the male, but he does not go so far as to think of them as real gods. God is in this context a force of universal unity and order personalised through the first ancestor – *unkulunkulu* (the very earliest progenitor). Anthropologists are often confused about the use of this metaphor and think that Zulu concepts of a universal creator go no further than their first ancestor. This and the charge that the Zulu God is only a vague idea, whether one believes in a god or not, are misconceptions arising from imposing individualistic concepts of god on a totally different system. A Zulu (traditionally) would ask – according to his habits of perceiving reality – 'Why should anyone be so definite about a god they have never seen?'

Zulu Poems

From the Ravages of Life we Create

And the suns are torn from the cord of the skies
And fall to the ground humiliated by the cluster of leaves.
The eternal feet travel on on their journey.
The bars of iron pierce through, feeding on their blood.
The wedding party walks proudly
And catches a glimpse of the moon disintegrating.
Beyond this aberration in the land of the hostile winds,
The tall woman is seized by madness.
She covers her face with a black cloth
Imitating the dance of the ecstatic children.
Then the ruined man of time fondles her
Until she gives birth, and gives birth to the infants of stone.
We are their kin whose ribs are wide with their power,
We are one with those who wander everywhere.
A man enters and marks down our generation
And tells us how suddenly summer has come
And makes us sing though our hearts are bleeding

Knowing how because of us,
We who are the locusts with broken wings,
Our shadows shelter the earth from the sun.

Thoughts at the Gathering of the Storm

The great smoker smokes wild hemp in the skies.
The smoke clouds move patiently
Giving life to a million images.
The axe-rays of the sun cut and pass.
There is no blood from the skulls.
They wander and assemble on the horizon

Until in their anger they are bound like gigantic knots.
They hurry back wiping out the centre of the sun.
The skies are torn with plural rains
The rains are tears that will remain with the earth.

We do not know when the world will end.
So we stand on an ant hill
Eulogising a thousand years
Saying tomorrow, there will be tomorrow
Suspended with our shadows on the clouds.
It is then that the great smoker of time
Will smoke again, in the abyss of the south.

In Praise of the Earth (extract)

I discovered you, great mystery curved on the sky.
The horizon stretches with the heritage of the sun.
Beyond infinity there is infinity,
The curled hand of imagination carries heavy gifts
Until the splash of the rain breaks into silence
And echoes with voices of generations:
They who are born from the ribs of the earth
And find the power to bloom on the fertile soil;
They who traverse the planet of voices;
How can their voices be heard?
How can their shadows embrace those of the mountain?
They will be folded under the great night.
Others who follow this path will not understand
How so many who loved you so much could die so easily.
You were the woman who fed all generations

Who still come forth throbbing like a giant heart,
But inside their bellies thrive the venomous scorpions.
How could you, a woman famed for her beauty,
Give birth to such ugliness?
The end of the cycle is the beginning of the cycle.
Years come carrying firewood on their heads
And meet the day alight with ferocious flames
Burning your breasts in their firmness
Leaving the lips to utter the curse.
These men know the violence of the vultures.

Beautiful one, stretch the umbrella of the sun
And allow us to pass in your parades
Singing in the afternoon with the blades of grass
Which sleep as we sleep and fertilise the earth.
It is then that our flesh will merge
Into the beautiful one, making our legends beautiful.

Wenishet-Jusmere

I imagine you walking on the broken sands
Late in the evening
With the splendour of the red veils in the horizon.
The beat shakes the ground at the mountain of shadows,
And people are following the sign of the pleiades.
I imagine the cloud coherent over the columns,
Hammers forgotten and retired to the earth
The swollen earth fat with dreams,
The night trembling in the shower of light.
I see you round and round the earth

Breaking the encasement of memory,
Eagles escaping from the tormented space.
You who are life to come
You who made the sun with tears
You who made Damascus
You whose hands are thin with silence
Take this hour and tell time
In the evening. . . .

Master of Days

In the centre of the centre of the centres
There is an old man
Whose body is one with us,
Who tore the locks of daylight
Unfolding his legs with all hours.
When he releases the day of triumph,
He will release it with fertilising leaves that are ourselves.

The Night

The heart of the earth is covered with weeds,
Darkness descends from the path of the skies.
The black tails of cows shake against the wind,

Beating the sea with the fence of dusk.
It is as if people crawl in the islands of the light:
He who was as tall as the forest
Creeps on his belly dancing in the embrace of a dream;
The wilderness of the earth holds its head in its hands.
The little children have fled to their holes:
The hole is a great home of the ancestral spirits
Where grief hangs above like ribs,
Where the great day sends its forerunners
The white hair, the white hair of the sun.
You will also carry the cripple across the streams.

Sons of Vulindlela

Happy are the sons of Vulindlela
Who are armed with swords of thought
Who cut the roots of an unknown plant
Who begin from the beginning of beginnings
Who upturn stones lurking with scorpions
Who shout at the running buck
Who return a hundred times with tales
Who stood stretched into the horizon
Who rushed above with a thousand years.
It is they who will not be shaken,
Who have no fear of the hostile winds.

Place of Dreams

There is a place
Where the dream is dreaming us,
We who are the shepherds of the stars.
It stands towering as tall as the mountains
Spreading its fire over the sun
Until when we take one great stride
We speed with the eagle on our journey.
It is the eagle that plays its wings on our paths,
Wakening another blind dream.
Together with other generations hereafter
They shall dream them like us.
When they wake on their journeys they will say:
Someone, somewhere, is dreaming us, in the ruins.

Man's Power over Things

I shall not release you from the rope of words
Binding you to the projection of stones,
Swinging you with all winds.
I'll wait until you dream a great dream
And stretch your hand to break its lions
Making them subordinate to your will,
Then slowly snap their backs, as I watch.
When you have drawn their last breath
I shall pull my sword and split the marrow of their bones
Making you see their emptiness,
No more will you hold your faith in things
But sing the greatness of your blood.

Triumph of Thought

So I put thoughts on the palm of your hand
And let the pleiades race in the sky;
Winter will try again to overwhelm us
But we shall be ready with the warmth of blood.
And you, in the company of twins, will shelter us.
Then she, the widowed leopard, will retreat into the hill
And there howl all night long.
She will walk about naked and destitute
Deprived of the glory of her victims.
You alone will triumph in your power.
The male calf will find its joy in the stampede
Beating the ground with its triumphant hoofs
Because it shall be the young bull of the earth.

For a Friend who was Killed in the War

SINGLE VOICE: In the sun-drenched cliffs of the evening
Where I bade my brother farewell.
GROUP: Birds beat their wings and turn away.
SINGLE VOICE: I should not have returned alive
GROUP: The heart weeps endlessly.
SINGLE VOICE: It would have been you facing this fatal grief.
ALL: The worlds have scars, the worlds weep.
SINGLE VOICE: Even the dreams that I dream fill me with fear.
ALL: The leopard devours whom it chooses,
It is now I experience the grief of widows.
SINGLE VOICE: How shall I report at the house of Somhlalela?
How shall I?

A Farewell

I who have sung you songs over the years
I depart.
The staff is broken
The young ebony plant sinks in the mud.
These winds are wailing with seeds.
They will scatter them on the open space
Where rains will give birth to jungles.
I believe in the great day
Which will make our paths meet:
I shall wake then from the desert
Seeing you approach with pots filled with water.
We shall sit at the place of the old man
Untying the knots in the expanse of the afternoon,
In the fertility of the fig tree
In the vastness of the willow tree
In the savannahs of the fleeting antelope.

After the Age of Pain

Other great pains may follow.
The season of the locust passes;
Then enters the age of the sterile ones,
Fools that rule from gigantic thrones
Deriving their joy from the words of dry leaves,
The leaves that spread their emptiness on the dry sand.
The earth will become fertile one day
And the islands will stretch to the horizons
Overgrown with fruits from the weeds.

If we die

How many deceive themselves
That when we are dead
They will tell the truth?
They accuse us of entangling them
By our presence over the fire,
Telling others: the logs that burn
Are our tears.
Even when we are departed
They shall for ever be restless in our empty houses
Accusing the chairs of harbouring our secrets
As if they loved us when we lived.
Their guilt shall pursue them
Driving them from wall to wall
Showing them those who come after us.
They will speak for us
Even though they did not know us
Because they shall be the fire in our eyes.

Time will come

Time will come
Bringing the gifts of her secrets.
These arms that are bound into infinity
Will kindle the flame of the volcano
Erupting with light onto our paths.
Imagination shall overpower the children of the sun
Making them burst forth with our tomorrows.
They shall give birth before their innocence has been consumed.

Cycle

Part I

So many are asleep under the ground,
When we dance at the festival
Embracing the earth with our feet.
Maybe the place on which we stand
Is where they also stood with their dreams.
They dreamed until they were tired
And handed us the tail with which we shall dance.
Even the weeds emerge in their praise.
Yesterday there were vast villages;
We too shall follow their path,
Our dust shall arise at the gathering place
And the child will dance alone on our grounds.

Part II

How many generations
We dance over
When we are happy at the feast.
They scream from the outskirts,
Where we shall not reach with our feet.
Our eyes break into the sea of the night
When we arrive at the disputed field
Where people fight for a resting place,
Competing with the generations of antiquity.
Their tried voices rise
Rising with their songs
That will remain after the festival.

Thought on June 26

Was I wrong when I thought
All shall be avenged?
Was I wrong when I thought
The rope of iron holding the neck of young bulls
Shall be avenged?
Was I wrong
When I thought the orphans of sulphur
Shall rise from the ocean?
Was I depraved when I thought there need not be love,
There need not be forgiveness, there need not be progress,
There need not be goodness on the earth,
There need not be towns of skeletons,
Sending messages of elephants to the moon?
Was I wrong to laugh asphyxiated ecstasy
When the sea rose like quicklime
When the ashes on ashes were blown by the wind
When the infant sword was left alone on the hill top?
Was I wrong to erect monuments of blood?
Was I wrong to avenge the pillage of Caesar?
Was I wrong? Was I wrong?
Was I wrong to ignite the earth
And dance above the stars
Watching Europe burn with its civilisation of fire,
Watching America disintegrate with its gods of steel,
Watching the persecutors of mankind turn into dust
Was I wrong? Was I wrong?

Elegy for my Friend E. Galo

You died without my knowing
When I was out collecting firewood
To roast the meat,
That we may dance over the earth,
Even with white fat oxen;
And dance, not caring for the shape of their horns.
You died without my knowing,
When I thought I would tell you stories
Saying 'once upon a time on the earth' –
Meaning we who are one with the years
Meaning the beating of the hearts
Beating against the muscles of their desires.
I bought them expensively with gold.
You died without my knowing
You covered me with shame
As I followed you,
Admonishing those who carried you
Not to imitate you
And say death is a common thing.
If it were true I would not be here,
I would not have known that locusts
Greedily reap the fields
Leaving the discordant symphony of naked stars.
It is these that wept over the centuries.

Presence

Sleep tries to split us apart
But dreams come and open our gates.
You descend with the sound of bells

And enter into the centre of a large house,
Playing with wild dogs.
I tear off the doors from the east
And throwing them into a great fire
They burn and light your face.
It is beautiful like a vast planet.
Your face turns as if to smile
But a distant voice calls you back
And you disappear without talking
Leaving the nostalgia of your image.

Abundance

I possess a thousand thundering voices
With which I call you from the place of the sinking sun.
I call you from the shaking of branches
Where they dance with the tail of the wind.
You are the endless abundance
Singing with the lips of all generations.
You are like a trunk lush with branches in the lake
Whom the feller of woods felled in vain,
But sprouts with new buds in summer.
When it is loaded with fruit he comes again
And eats to saturation desiring to end its season;
But again and again the branches shoot forth with new seasons.

Images

Great houses harboured their heritage,
Distributing it to the young chickens.
Now the vast hands are empty,
Beating the shells in the sands,
Making voluminous sounds
That echo like a thousand violins.
The winds of summer interlock with the long wails of winter.
They salute the old ruins at the uncompleted foundations,
Unveiling the knots of skulls,
The sockets that laughed on the journey of the sun.
The praise-name is replaced by new generations
Who live near the festival.
Those in the dust are deprived of dawn
The heritage belongs to those beyond these fields.

In Memory of a Fanatic

Almost a thousand years ago.
Your tears are dry on a stone,
Your perfumes are commingled with dust.
What was the use of this death?
Those who saw your gigantic arm across the skies
Spreading the inscriptions of faith
Were the locusts on the dry fields of maize
Who let their wings flutter from age to age,
Who carried the fire with their lips,
Singeing your long hair in the wind.
They bent their faith according to the times.

Mother Earth, or the Folly of National Boundaries

Why should those at the end of the earth
Not drink from the same calabash
And build their homes in the valley of the earth
And together grow with our children?

Isle of Man Christmas 1967

How can I be silent
Over the mountains of Theleni
Hearing sweet sounds extending to the ends of the world,
Hearing the scattered voices of children
Carried by the echo in the valleys
Which summons them on the staff of the morning –
Where I shall see them beautiful
Having grown and flowered?
The mysterious event is this very one
That I grow up with them always.
Now I dance with a tall bird
Which spreads its wings
And surrounds the wide earth,
Laying its eggs on the nest
Where a great day will emerge
And intertwine with another long day,
Making a pendant with the song that pursues me.
It will be joyful at the fields of the dry stalks
Whom new thundering steps break the springs,
And the happy daughters of Jabulile will not die.

Feet of Men

Path in the sand,
Whose feet are these that lead to the shade
Criss-crossed in all directions?
Each time I follow them they end in the forest.
Then I look up to the sky
Searching their mystery.
I see shadows returning home in the afternoon.
When I am left alone with the night,
I hear voices babbling
With the wisdom of other nations.
I approach them:
Suddenly they stop with the wind –
Then I hear footsteps striking the hours.

Depressing Thoughts about Man

Mother of the skies,
The eggs on which you sit
Have decayed.
The earth emits the stench of your rotten yolk.
The nestlings that escaped
Are equipped with sharpened claws;
They are killing each other.
Even you, Simungulu, you are silent
Feeding the hunger of your ancient eyes with laughter.
Sisholo knows us:
We are the ants that devour each other
On the flatness of the stone.

Peace

Sing again the great song,
Sing it with the winds that are shaking the reeds.
Sing until the whole earth is shaken by the song.
Maybe summer may yet come again.
They summon you, who stand at the ruins.
They praise your once great kingdom,
Teeming with free men.
Across, in the villages devastated by war, they are calling
Saying: 'Come you who broke the battle axe,
Men are cutting men on the river bed.'
The waters that ran with the rainbow
Are curled with clots of blood;
The new seedlings sprout no more.
But you who speak with a dream
You will visit us
And unveil the new age
Letting us sleep on our backs
Listening to the multitudes of the stars.

A Poem

May I when I awake
Take from all men
The yearnings of their souls
And turn them into the fountain of Mpindelela
Which will explode into oceans;
Not those of the south that are full of bitterness
But those that are sweet to taste.

At the Place of Death

Nothing returns from the place of Mathulela,
Even voices burn in the sun.
When they thrust their arrows
They pierce through the stomach of the buck
And flee in their great fear,
Dying on the cliffs overhung with rocks.
There they are hanging on their broken limbs;
They cry no more.
They are silent with a palpitating silence.
In vain the calves scream,
Nondaba runs alone in an ecstasy of prophecies
Running on the desert as huge as the ruins
She cries out: 'O suns give birth to a place better than ours.'

To the Killer

If your species multiply
And all men derive from your image,
We shall open our doors
Watching them sharpening their swords with the morning star
And spreading their blades covered with blood.
They shall obstruct our passage in our travels
And cut our heads because we were of alien clan,
Believing that our blood is desirable.
But the growing of the powerful buds
Will not let them triumph;
They will haunt them with talons of weeds
Piercing them in their dreams.

When I looked back

I am haunted by your nostalgia,
You who reaped the flesh,
You whose paths cry with pain,
You who have power over the skulls of the earth.
I miss you even in the night of barren women,
I wait in vain for your shadow.
When I find it intertwined in my fingers
I open the door eagerly
Thinking you may emerge.
I search for you in the piles of the dead.
I do not find you.
This great nostalgia
Attacks me in the midst of bats.
I rushed like a wounded bird until I was silent
Under the buildings of those greater than you.
Perhaps it was my ghost fears
That made you tower above me.
Perhaps I was in the company of inferior men.

Man

May I divorce myself from philosophers
Who stand detached from the affairs of men,
Who turn their hearts into clay.
I had met men I despised
But it was they who made the cauldron of the earth,
Alone raised the star,
Surpassing the glory of the sun.

To the Soldier Hero

Who was Langula
That he should trample over a thousand victims
And praise himself over their graves?
Is it not true: for him there was only one great joy –
To hold the iron dripping with their blood,
As though this fame
Fulfills all life's ambition?
But even he who sharpened the edge of hearts
Conceived new truths,
Telling us that truth is not the truth of swords,
But the long buds growing from the ruins.

Tree of Life

Beautiful tree of Jomela,
You sheltered us from northern winds
And devoured little plants.
You stood alone on the hill-top
Where the afternoon dances with its red feathers.
You swayed with a million years.
When the eagle settled on the pinnacles
It found us where we slept
And chased us with dreams.
We shall see its eyes burning with death
Whilst you stand firm to eternity
Counting our years.
When you scatter the leaves
You scatter them where we perish.

Tribute to Joan Baez on Vietnam

Mshengu, mother of dawn,
You who traversed the hills of the Ethiopians
And returned with a dream,
Spread your wings over the girl's stone
And sing a great song at the waterfalls;
Feed it with the gourds of your breasts
When they burst above the day,
May they be the heritage of the generation of Nkulu
Because you alone, whose heart is vast,
You distributed hearts from the islands.

The Power of Past Regrets

Awake let us go to the end of the world
Where we shall hear the winds at dawn
Arriving after seeking us over a thousand years.
When we hear them speaking over the reeds
We shall ask their names: they shall tell us
They are the voice of Vuyisile
Carrying us their pleasant tales.
So life is:
Beautiful things are the abandoned vessels.
Even these endless talkers
Tell us tales of great things of yesterday.
In their regrets they incantate:
'Were we at the stone of Ntunjambili
It would open its gates and embrace us.'
They mourn even though they never reached its sacred grounds.

The Screams

I offer you screams of a thousand mad men
Who scream to those without mercy
Who scream over the graveyards
Of skeletons, piled on piles,
Bones dislocated from their joints.

I offer you voices of a thousand vultures
Who hover over fields of flesh
Where columns abandon columns in the hills
Where the eyes are lost in the sockets
Where the moon abandons them in the wilderness.

I offer you the cloth that is torn in the middle,
Left in the field
By those who departed before the children were weaned from the
    breast.
Tell me, tell me,
Who wore it before the fall of winter?

I offer you those who sleep alone
With their hands folding the dream,
A dream that will never come
Because they stare in the night of death,
I offer them to you to shout them to the world!

Others

When I have fulfilled my desires
Let me take these grain baskets,

And fill them up with other men's desires,
So that whoever crosses the desert
May never starve.

Aloneness

Whoever climbs the Khahlamba mountains
Knows how lonely is loneliness,
Beating its echoing sounds on the pinnacles of the stones,
Stretching its dry tongue,
Searching for warmth in the ribs of the night,
And turning the empty gourds
Whistling with absent shadows.

He is alone who is alone,
Who is with a child wailing in the sand
Left by the wayside in a great famine.
The mother consoled herself saying 'Whoever finds it
Will embrace it within their families.'
Though nursed with love
It will ever be alone,
Ignorant of the breast of heaven.
The elephants that are the walls of the earth
Are burdened with echoes,
Imprisoned in the umbilical cord of the earth.

Friends

Honey are the words you speak
Whilst I drift slowly into sleep.
You tell the story over and over again.
I drowse in the palm of your hand
Whilst you hold the body aching with pain.
Softly you cover it
And whisper in my ear.
Although knowing I do not hear you,
You do it for the heart
Which alone never sleeps.

Two Wise Men

ALL: What news do you bring us O Magalela?
ONE: I bring news from the villages of Mfolozi river.
ALL: What do they say at Mfolozi O Magalela?
ONE: They say it is you who know great secrets.
ALL: What great secrets do they want us to tell O Magalela?
ONE: The story of Zongwana the son of Mbiya.
ALL: Yes we do know Mbiya, we do know Zongwana.
ONE: Come and tell me when the sun is setting
ALL: We have never seen the sun ever since their departure.
    The sun was they who made the epics,
    Who said war should tread carefully in this world,
    Who said mankind has one great song,
    Who said the great ones are those whose songs belong to
      all men.
ONE: Yes: it is these who created our visions.

Elegy for Msizi

O Msizi son of Thulini,
Have you ever seen crowds mourning at the Khahlamba
   mountains,
Trampling on each other under the shadow of the mountains,
The voice of Senzeni the son of Zemila tormented by grief?
Have you ever heard voices confronting each other
With mumbled tales,
Men with softened eyes drenched with tears
Until the winds spread with the night?

People are as numerous as the fields.
People are as numerous as the grass,
Their fate follows with the wind.
Their lives are dogged by sadness.

The shadow of Gedeni is following me
We accompanied him
Saying to the soil of Vczindaba 'be fertile'
And let grow a great tree of the Bhele clan.

The child of man enters
And throws the mourning cloth on the ground
Saying 'Mother do you hear the voice
Wailing as if to fill the whole earth?'
Happy is the woman who has no child,
Who has not fed the sterile earth,
Happy is the Tukela river which sings with all the years
Picking and spitting sands on the shores.

I find the great tree grown.
It has grown from the nourishment of the son of Thulini.
The old wind is coming to blow the seeds.
They will emerge as the vast forests on the sea shore.

Invocation to Life

Flute player,
You play in perpetual motion,
You who are the turbulence of the forests.
You stripped them of their leaves
Until the wind came and whistled on them.
Nomina, your mother, summons you,
She summons you with rivers
And calls you to the dancing place
Where people play under the half-moon;
Shadows mingle in their ecstasy.
Nomanjalo your companion awaits you.
The song will swell and fill the earth,
Your fame will echo among all lovers,
And you and she will walk the universe
Making all planets sing in one anthem
Because you are the heritage of all life.

Diplomacy

Have you ever seen the rulers of this earth
Hugging before great assemblies,
Reverberating with words before the excited crowds,
In all these displays hiding long knives
Staring each other in the roots of their eyes?
Then one day out of this glorious peace
The cliffs resound with cries of war
Each tearing the skies with thunderous fury
Abusing the witch they once embraced.

Stages of Existence

I watched the rainbow
Advancing with the faces of old women
Who raised their heavy eyes
Like the shadows of magical figures.
I bent the rainbow-rope from the horizon
So that I might tie the earth
So that whatever is passed of the past
May give birth.
Beyond the red boundaries
Is the new lightning of children
Who will grow above
The shadows of old women.
When they have conquered them
They may rest and create new forms
That inspire new life
Making knots for eternity
From which new generations will arise . . .

Time and Change

Time does not move.
It stands fixed in the centre of the earth.
Only the lips talk.
The watchman equipped with a thousand eyes
Stands hypnotized without my mysteries of change.
He would laugh a statuesque laughter
Because in that deep night he stands alone
Ineffective in the moment of history.

Bomb Threat

In that moment I loved you life
Letting you down on my arms
So that I may indulge you in my embrace
In spite of the brute-men
Who wanted to take you away from me.

My breast swelled with milk to feed you.
I deceived myself
In that moment of death, when I call
I'll find you still loving me.

The mushroom of death
Whispered: 'Those like you
Who love life must know I come slowly.'
I watched out in the streets
And saw crowds exchanging their salutations.

I stayed in that dark house joking with you,
Strengthening my wooden plate on which I eat,
So that you may not touch the innocent,
The children who grew up not knowing your name
But speaking your language.

To Prince Magena

In that moment of your downfall
You were as beautiful as red iron thongs.
You were like an ancestral spirit,
Your eyes sparked with lightning.

I used to hate you in your conceit
When you swelled high like a mountain
Boasting with the boom of drums
Which your followers endlessly beat.

I used to watch you splashing
The mud of your heart
Into the lilies,
The men who walk the earth.

Today I approached you
And found you humbled like an old dog.
I watched your eyes
And heard the hymn of life rumbling.

Then I knew
Even the weeds that grow in the field
Flower and emit their scent,
Like you, you who are the shell of your power.

On the Death of Young Guerillas

You called me, but I made no response in that night;
I feared you, you whose power strikes with terror.
You killed my children with a blunt spear,
You held me back so that I may not bury them.
The soil disgorges them:
Wherever I go I find their bodies scattered.
Could it be that you are tired of the old ones
Who reappear in the valley of dreams?
Could it be they whet your appetite with their flesh?
Could it be you are blind in your destruction?

The Power of Creativity

The sea echoes in the caves
Celebrating its conquest into the darkness,
Exploding from the belly of the earth
Until the giant bulls are awakened from their sleep.
They cry till their voices split the moon.
Blood flows into the blanket of the skies
Congealing into coils of mist.
Your power struts on the cliffs like a gorilla.
You return having conquered the earth.
I know, because dawn advances,
You will never be conquered by cowards.
You will break their fortress
Releasing the leaf that has long been buried,
Making it quiver on the shore of great waves,
Kindling the lips that have long been silent.

To the Watcher of the Gates

Watcher of the gates of life
Let me enter with my children
To sing within great anthems.
We have long promised, on the wings of the eagle,
That we shall break open the skies
And release the wild horses of heaven.
They will dance and run in the wide east,
While we with our dreams hold onto them
Until we arrive at the end of the world.
We shall enter a million great villages
And tell those within great tales;

They will not again awake with grief,
But will emerge with the rays of the sun
Playing to us their songs.
Alas! It is you mother of Nomavimbela who holds us back,
You make us uncertain with your long shadows.
When we have merged
We shall create one world, a world full of epics.

The Sweet Voice

Your sweet voice rises with the wind into the sky
Singing songs with the swallows.
The emptiness of the feast returns,
Imploring you to teach others to fly;
Then waves upon waves will take to their wings
Until the umbilical cord of heaven is rent
With unending symphonies.

The Civilisation of Iron

I saw them whose heads were shaved,
Whose fingers were sharpened, who wore shoes,
Whose eyes stared with coins.

I saw them
In their long processions
Rushing to worship images of steel:
They crushed the intestines of children
Until their tongues fell out.
I saw iron with sharp hands
Embracing infants into the flames.
They wandered on the roads
Preaching the religion of iron,
Pregnant with those of blood and milk.
I saw milk flowing
Like rivers under the feet of iron.
The earth shrank
And wailed the wail of machines.
There were no more people,
There were no more women,
Love was for sale in the wide streets
Spilling from bottles like gold dust.
They bought it for the festival of iron.
Those who dug it
Curled on the stones
Where they died in the whirlwind.
I saw the worshippers of iron
Who do not speak.

Over the Cities

The twin red moon
Watches over the skies of the cities
Flirting with shadows of the night.

The earth heaves
Releasing great ants,
That climb the walls of the ruins.
The space of the eagle
Watches over the centuries.
It is as if only you, Nokuthula, is silent,
You who hoard all gifts.
You see the cycle turning slowly,
Then you collect tales of unending planets
And set them into great flames
Making their images turn with long shadows.
The flesh of the flesh revolving and turning
While the salamanders watch the centuries.

Repeat

The substance of knowledge
Is a circular pot bursting with abundance
On which many lips are feeding.
When they have satisfied their appetites
They place it delicately at the sacred place,
So that even in the time of famine
We may recall its sweetness
And know that hunger will pass
Because greatness ever repeats itself.

The Valley of Rest

You the carved earth who was made for our dreams,
We the orphans of Ndabandabeni,
Come as crowds of tired travellers.
We come to wipe off our journey's sweat
So that you may relieve us of their pains.

Sizwile may have deceived us,
Waiting on us when we despaired,
Telling us when we go beyond these arid regions
There is the love of those who know us.

Because we saw you with the sadness
That surrounded us everywhere
We were afraid, afraid lest
The hunger of our dreams
May eat and never fill.

But the retreating hills
Overlooking the ruins of our hearts,
Show, with dancing power, the moments to come.
We shall take their excitement and say
We shall persist as long as they do not mock us with their spiralled
    dreams.

The ecstasy in the dream
Accompanies us on the sand,
Rushing to reap the fruit cultivated like us.
It returns to feed with us without end.

Why should not man,
After he is born, know what is to come
And rid himself of the dust of hopes
And move with the beating of the heart?
Why should he grope in the dark?

Unlike you, great valley,
Who are like the flowers we saw
Dryly falling on the naked earth
Until they fertilised the dunes of desert dust.

You are as great as your songs.
We shouted them everywhere
Saying we who started on the horizon
Are now the sons of the valley of Mbuyamanzi.

A Great Generation

OTHERS: When shall Mathungo and Bhekani return
        So long ago they departed, promising their return the
        day after?
ONE: They will return
        When the walls thunder with beetles.
OTHERS: What holds them in this long absence?
ONE: It is the days obstructing them in their return,
        Blocking the gates in the land of setting suns;
        Demanding from them the fruit of life.
OTHERS: Where will they find it, since the world decays with the
        years?
ONE: It is they alone who hold the truth.
ALL: They will bring life to a great generation,
        A generation that will rise from the ruins.
ONE: I hug their deafness in the dark
        The voices begin to speak their first syllables
        Giving their messages.

c

Grain of Antiquity

Night of night of nights in antiquity
A new plant grows from your seed,
Flowering with life from the grains of the earth.
The breast pants on the reeds of the river,
Releasing the voice that is life.
The song has no end;
Dry stalks will not die,
But will raise their lips
Tearing another season with their fertility.
The shepherds who stand guard at the curves of the earth
Count the villages, leaving others to generations to come
Saying, 'It is not we alone who have the power of the flesh.'

Tribute to Rodin

I am pure with the purity of the star.
Its fire follows the infinity of the mind.
Wild lilies open their petals on the footprints,
Beating their wings like legendary dragons.
This agony makes mystery-cycles of mists.
I saw you turning aside
And setting alight a pile of firewood
Whose flames forged men
Who wandered, giving birth to other mysteries.
When the fire diminished with its flames
Smooth limbs emerged with their hands outstretched
And their lips open to speak with an echo
Stepping their tall feet to the sky.

People

As I live so do you live,
Because you are part of my existence.
If I inherited you with my knowledge
Then I would possess an ever-living ancestral spirit
Bound to other worlds.
When I have severed the umbilical cord
I still recognise the burial ground,
Since this essence echoes my experience.
Likewise the multitudes of my multitudes
Are the multiples of those that have known,
And bequeath the particles of their existence.

Vengeance

How would it be if I came in the night
And planted the spear in your side
Avenging the dead:
Those you have not known,
Those whose scars are hidden,
Those about whom there is no memorial,
Those you only remembered in your celebration?
We did not forget them.
Day after day we kindled the fire,
Spreading the flame of our anger
Round your cities,
Round your children,
Who will remain the ash-monuments
Witnessing the explosions of our revenge.

The Idealist

Son of Mhlaleli, it is you who caused me this restlessness.
You sent me on a futile journey to chase the moon,
Making me wander after the galloping horses of the world.
I tried to lure the moon with whistling
While stubbornly it hovered over my forehead.
I stood at the end of the earth
Supported by the hero's staff.
Insistently I followed the milky way with the dreams of the
     Sibhekedu river.
We were promised, we who worshipped zealously,
We were to inherit the abundance of slow maturing years.
But how long must we wait with so little time?

At the War Monument

We were waiting at the monument
In the centre of a great city decked with images.
Patiently the sun rose
Beating the sky with its broken wings.
When the ceremony was over, and the splendid rituals,
We heard from within the song of a Tibetan shepherd
Echoing through the earth.
Time with its diabolic fears wrenched our shadows.
To appease her we sang together
But we know now, together means death.
It was so easy to die then
Knowing dying has received the sacrificial young bulls.
A new era begins with its purity of blood:
The ocean beats on the rocks like a long line of stars.

The Cruel Beast

The man-spider hangs on a dry log
Shaking his hair and making the night.
The raised skin is hard.
The beast approaches
Wanting to crush us in its teeth.
At first to appease him, we sacrificed our son,
But his appetite is sharpened by our flesh.
He sits contented over the bones.
Because of him orphans weep,
Crossing the paths we have passed.
It is here that the hard eyes burn with fire.
The footsteps encircle us like a murderous crowd
Directing the sharpness of the spear
Making it run into our ribs.
The ribs are twisted, they do not speak
Silenced by the hands of the beast.

To the Complaining

He utters these complaints
Who has not seen miseries
Beginning to give birth
Profuse like a woman who gives birth to twins.
Not knowing he is not alone in the night
He cuddles the words of the cradle
Which are a million desires.
He is one with those who depart with the wind
Who hang onto the nests of swallows.

Image of the Earth (Life)

World of Dlinza,
What is the mysterious thing you carry
Which made you swell like a hunch back?
Your ribs are folded in the valley.
Here is a great bird beating its wings;
Patiently waiting to give us cause to mourn
It will descend to tear our skulls.
Underneath the soft belly
The bowels are scattered,
Harbouring a calf that was not born with others.
Alone it lives in a disfigured world,
How else would the cripples have survived among the vultures?

The Bond

Gumede son of Ndaba, here I am.
I have come to present
This grinding stone of Masilela, my mother.
It is heavy, as though she weighted it with magic.
She left on it the gourd of her heart.
Do not forget it at Mpembeni house
Lest the vermin multiply on it.
Life may put a curse on us
Since we did not behave like her children.
If he be present who has a thousand ribs
Do not allow him to deceive you,
Promising a place for it on the fertile lands.
Hold it sacred knowing in it is our soul.

Restlessness and Experience

I loved Nomaphakade
Though she made me wander with the winds,
Persecuting me,
Making me taste the bitter herb.
Had I sat contented
I would have died the death of anthills,
Where swallows dance on the mound.
I place her among the immortals
Who are the multitudes in our history.
I ask her not to leave me
But let me reap this experience.

Peace

Smooth boulders hang over deep pools.
Many shadows sink into the dream.
They slip into their death
Failing to grasp the vessel
That is suspended on the wave.
They drown without tasting the sweetness of peace.
Peace floats silently.
The boy who wanders finds it
And lifts it to the sun
Making the thirsty travellers drink
To multiply and fill the earth.

To the Reluctant Poetess: Alicia Medina

Daughter of the daughter of the skies
What song in this world is without tears?
Even those that rise with the rainbow
Emerge from ground infested with decay.
Do not spend your days on the ground
But rise with the swallow into the sky.
It is then that you will know:
These great songs echo from the caves with tears.
It is they alone that feed the crowd at the break of day
Saturating them with potent tongues.
So must you leave the place of innocence
And offer to the winds your heart.
Then the blind will sing to the earth
Thundering simultaneously with immortal rivers.
With them the great plants will flower again;
And those who are tired find a shade to rest
And eat the fruits of their greatness.

The Spectacle of Youth

I loved the children of the lion
When their manes were beginning to grow,
Simulating the ancient heroes.
I knew the greatness of their future
When they leapt on the tender necks of antelopes
Which so long prided themselves on their fleetness.
I praised the skilfullness of their power,
Knowing how soon they will be killing buffaloes.

The Voice of the Night

Each time I provoke your voice
I hear the wailing in the long night,
Carrying a screaming child on its back,
Going round the wide world.
I struggle with my fears, hoping it will be silent
And find its resting place.
But its unending cry sears my mind.
You called: 'Even the dances that you play
Will not make me silent.'
In you is the end of the cycle,
The final voice of the afternoon.

The Dance

I hear the drums in the afternoon,
Voices throng at the dancing place.
Today we are singing the songs of Bayise.

The great dancer quivers with the wind
And asks me, the spectator,
'Who is silent whilst others sing?'
I answer 'It is Daliyeka.'

I know him who is silent,
Who is the voice of the earth,
Who will remain alone repeating our names
When we lie buried in the forest,
Perpetuating us in the memories of man.

c*

Dedication

When you have crossed the river
Search for a fertile place.
There prepare the ground
And plant the seeds of our desire.
Plant it for the generations of summer
Who when they arrive will reap the harvest
And be filled with our fruit.
They will remember us in their tales
Saying this pleasure is mine and Ndondoshiya's
Meaning him and a thousand years.

Realisation

Do you remember a great night
When the earth was filled with hunting dogs?
You promised then to forgive the moon,
As it rose from the Msunduze river;
When it attempted to drink from the earth
Wild dogs chased and devoured it.
Do you remember?
When we heard the voices of men we ran to them
Wanting to know who they were.
When we called they were silent.
When we found they were the echoes of our youth
We took the shorter journey
Announcing the festivals across the streams.
Then we knew we did not inhabit this earth alone:
People emerged, animals emerged, and the sun. . . .

An Elegy to the Unknown Man nicknamed Donda the Son of Gabela, who died in the War

Underneath the shade of the *mnqanawe* plants
There is a black stone.
It stands memorial to Donda son of Gabela.
It is him alone, the child of men, whom I loved.

I wandered on the impoverished hill,
Asking the elephant which way to go.
It shook the trees with its trunk
Pointing its head to the place of the setting sun.

What shall I do?
The place of the setting sun is asleep.
However, I try to wake its head;
I hear only the aching of dry skins.

I shall carry his bracelet
To sell it amongst those who shake the birds from their dreams,
Telling them to wake and wail again.
I shall build a mountain to rest my head.

Only then shall I boast with him,
Dancing over the wide spaces.
The stranger who passes, seeing us
Will ask 'Who is it that weeps on my path?'

Europe

Europe, your foundations
Are laid on a rough stone.
Your heart is like cobwebs
That are dry in the desert.

Your children fill us with fear:
They are like the young of a puff adder
Who devour the flesh of their parent.

Once I believed the tales.
Once I believed you had breasts
Over-flowing with milk.

I saw you rushing with books
From which the oracles derive their prophesies.
I heard you in the forest
Crying like wolves,
Breaking the bones of your clans.

I know the hardness of your visions:
You closed the doors
And chose the bridegroom of steel.

You chose her not to love
But because she alone remained
Dedicated to silence.

From her you made your prophecies
And summoned the oracles:
You laughed at the blind men
But you yourself were blind,
Struggling in this great night.

Children have inherited the fire.
They blow its flames to the skies

Burning others in their sleep.

What will the sun say?
The sun will laugh
Because it burnt out cradles from age to age.

Exile

Our lives were ruined
Among the leaves.
We decayed like pumpkins
In a mud field.

Sadness on a Deserted Evening

O Mantantashiya
Your child is crying
Alone, after the devastation of the earth.
Listen to it departing
With all the lion winds
That are pierced with spears.

Continuity

May it be so:
Let the great vessel be lifted from the ground
And the warm lips drink from it
Until the tongue begins to speak,
And spreads its song.
When thirst burns the mind
May we return again to the villages
Where we shall partake in a feast
With those that are no more.

Three Worlds

I stayed between two inaccessible planets,
One dead in a chasm of centuries,
Peopled with past men and dinosaurs,
Breeding time with visions of death.

I saw the other in the tears of an afternoon
Young, tender, and struggling from the womb
Tormented by the titanic images of dawn
In the gulf of the night, of rising stars.

I stood on the third world,
Bitter, neither young nor old
Heaving and heaving like a volcano,
Multiplying with fire:
I was all things.

Triumph of Man
(on looking at sculpture)

At the sculptured face in the shadow of the stone
The angle turns with the vision of the flesh.
Even he who created from the essence lives.
He fought the claws of the eagle
Knowing how often it rose swollen with pride.
He overcame this moment of time
Making the silent speak.
The ages babble with the sound of eternity.
The dead awake and frolic in a dance
Crushing the leaves that are daily scattered,
Because their faces have eyes,
And lips, and flesh, in the centuries.
The face that stands erect above the earth
Will turn its eyes, and plant its ears into time,
Listening to the rising epic of the years,
The years that boast with the ages of men
Who alone created eternity.

The Middle of the Cycle

There is no day passing
Without the barking of wild dogs.
They scream on the cliffs
While we slowly close our gates.
We ask ourselves: how long
Shall we escape their perpetual hunger?

The Sin of Monolithic love

My love committed a crime
And loved diminutive loves,
Yielding itself to die
Holding clay-pots of its drunkenness.

The advice of disreputable men
Led me to sit on the confines of a traditional stool.
They told me it is customary to face the fire
Watching identical shadows turning into mirages.

No one man
Is the single plant of the soil.
All men have their scars
For which other men seek their cure.

Those whose minds are centred on a sacred stone
Offering their limbs of existence,
Are destined for the rebuffs of life.
They will die in the thickets of reeds.

They shall weep on a pile of rubble
Which they have accumulated with dry hopes
While the abundance of harvest multiplies;
Everywhere grains of love sprouting in their fruitfulness.

Conquest of Dawn

At the tall mountain of the sun
I climbed the precipice
Battling with scorpions.
The sun laughed at me as it emerged from the womb
And unveiled the world of *mambas*.
I saw them hustling in the fields.
I cried to Mbenzi the prophetess
Believing she hears all our plight;
Not the plight of cowards
But the struggles of brave men.
She danced to me across the streams
While I hung on to the periphery of the stone
Seeing others before me drowning.
My father who is as great as the elephant
Gave me the eulogies of conquerors.
Even the winds
I have overcome.
I burned like the centre fire of the milky way.
Others below me sharpened their spears.
I composed my own great song
Armed against dawn.
It shall not again run over my shadow,
It shall not tear the skin of the lion,
It shall not find me dreaming, tomorrow.

Your Footprints

Your footprints were fearful.
They trampled over the dreaming earth.
But when you arose

You dragged broken legs,
Wailing like a cripple.
I stood aside watching you,
And saw you trembling.
Then I knew the mask of your cowardice had been removed.
You ran into the knot of the night
Blind in the direction of death
Until I found you and closed your eyelashes.

Suddenly we lost

As you were present at the dancing place
Hearts were beating,
Flowering with new fruits;
People were picking them at the great harvest.

Great singers shouted at the celebration,
Thundering anthems for the suspended rocks;
The wings of winter were broken,
Rivers burst thrusting high waves.

Until the hour of the strange night,
When the cunning mongoose
Broke our spine –
We who were swept by our treacherous ecstasies!

Gifts without a Recipient

Where were you the day we arrived with Nomalizo
Coming to bring ours and others' gifts?
Why did you not leave the imprints of your hands
So that we may count the fingers of the years,
Saying he has not departed like a river
Which leaves with the silence of death.
Alas! You left ruins as big as mountains
Haunted by the hubbub of bats,
Who mocked us with their wings.

Puzzle, or Man the Despicable Animal

One, I have kept great loves
Two, but few desired them
Three, the few were greedy ones
Four, how I hated them!

Therefore I have let this great love
Decay at the sacred place.
One day
The rats will emerge bloated with the feast
And celebrate the conquest of the earth.

They will give birth to men
Who will dance with the violence of thunder,
Proud of the maternity of rats,
Kindred with all ugliness.

Brief Beauty

In your beauty
I found sockets of death and retreated
Until I fell into chasms
That are collapsing
While the sun explodes with its flash of dawn.
It is as if it laughs with the centuries.
Mother of beautiful things
You shook the earth
Deceiving it with your illusions.
Your lips are ever
Proclaiming the end of man's life.

The Beggar

When you stared at me
With the recesses of your eyes
From which the dust of the field scatters
I saw empty wooden platters in your eyes.
I saw your thin hands shaking
As if their vibrations will germinate on all things.
You were in the wild inaccessible night
Your lips were breaking
Unaccustomed to uttering warm words.
A wild ant ran on your rags.
When you tried to break the words,
Their pieces fell apart asking to be fed.
Then I realised you were Mavuso.

The Political Prisoner

I desired to talk
And talk with words as numerous as sands,
The other side of the wire,
The other side of the fortress of stone.

I found a widow travelling
Passing the prisoners with firewood.
It is this woman who forbade me to sleep
Who filled me with dreams.

The dream is always the same.
It turns on an anchor
Until it finds a place to rest:
It builds its cobwebs from the hours.

One day someone arrives and opens the gate.
The sun explodes its fire
Spreading its flames over the earth,
Touching the spring of mankind.

Behind us there are mountains
Where the widow is abandoned.
She remains there unable to give birth
Priding herself only in the shadows of yesterdays.

The Gold-miners

Towers rise to the skies,
Sounds echo their music,
Bells ring backwards and forwards
Awakening the crowds from the centre of fire.
Attendants at the feast glitter,
Wealth piles on the mountains.
But where are the people?
We stand by watching the parades
Walking the deserted halls
We who are locked in the pits of gold.

Kindness

I waited for the restlessness
Of your hands
Holding all harvests of love.

At dawn
You walked in the wide fields of men
Who held you in their embrace.

You returned to the waiting crowds
Offering each one
His full vessel.

Uneasy Love

I washed my hands
In the pool where you washed your body
And listened to your voice in the darkness
Saying come back to me Masilela
Come back you who is loved.

The Day of Treachery

Do not be like the people of Ngoneni
Who rushed with warm arms
To embrace a man at the gates
And did likewise on the day of treachery
Embracing the sharp end of the short spears.

And Us

From the time the moon was ripe
We meet you departing and returning.
We say 'Make us provisions at the cairns
And pick our grindstone
Making it lie on others.'
People will know of us from them
Setting the flame of your love at the gates.
When you sit under the darkness
You will hear the echoes of our feet
Dancing the song.

On the Star Necklace

Great joy who possesses a million hearts,
Doves echo their voices across the lakes.
They sing to each other overwhelmed with ecstasy.
You have no limits.
You come with tell-tale vessels
Until, when we drink from them,
We fall into deep sleep and dream stars.
Each one collects his own cluster
And plaits them into necklaces
With which he shall boast,
Saying, these are my days;
And jealous ones stare in amazement.

Dedication to a Poet

Great poet, who sleeps between the rocks,
Your sleep is beautiful when the earth echoes
With the feet of men
Who break the ground to fill your place.
You left them, cups overflowing with sweetness.
They drink and return again and again
Climbing the hill entangled with thorns
Until they stand on the open space
Shouting your name,
Presenting your beauty
To each generation that reawakens with your song.

Anthem of Decades *(Extract from an epic)*

Part I

And then time was born:
The millepede-darkness encircled the earth
And silence surged into space like a pregnant moon.
Tufts of darkness entangled in the horizon
Making the earth heave like a giant heart.
The crooked mountains await the first fruit of the sun.
Whilst the night triumphed, the stars thrust their swords of light,

(Which, the tale goes, were worlds older than ours)
Tearing the black blanket with its hidden mysteries.
The creator who created heaven and earth
Filled this planet with the commotion of beasts
And walked the great path of the skies,
Looking on the hungry chasms of the mountains,
The racing of great rivers and spacious oceans
Whose waves beat eternally on the vast shores.

The belly of the earth split open
Releasing animals that crawl on the earth
And others that fly with their wings
And others that drum their hoofs on the ground.
The lion roared thundering the first fear.
Other beasts less ferocious stared
Until, aware of the satisfying taste of blood,
Joined in the general carnage.
So the lesson was learnt. Life must continue
And good things must feed the ruthlessness of appetites.

At the beginning the creator had messengers
Whom he sent to the ends of the universe:
Sodume, the Intelligence of Heaven,
Who explored the labyrinths of the earth
And opened the gates to all the creatures that inhabit the earth.

Satisfied with this work
He sang as they paraded
'These multitudes will fill this world of stone
The forests will be stampeding with wild animals
The mountains will be gambolling with antelopes
The overflowing rivers will be pregnant with life.
But in all this man is yet to come,
Proud and defiant before all things.'
So over and over he repeated the ecstasy of heaven
Like him who sings alone the anthems of life.

There was Simo who stood guard
At the limits of the universe,
Who blotted out, at intervals, the light of the moon
And darkness would return to the earth hoping to regain its lost
    territory.
He travelled often accompanied by the children of Sodume.
The wild ones who loved best
To flash the forks of lightning.
Their father Sodume lived near the earth
Where he played games with his wife Nodume.
She screamed, echoing her voice across the path of the sky.
But Sodume's voice, round and powerful, shook the heavens.
Often he emerged with her in relentless pursuit.
Both cherished the bluebird of heaven
Whose tail was deep blue, whose wings were blue
Whose body was blue but whose feet were of burning red.
Wherever they were they let it fly before them like a cloud.

Sometimes it would spread its wings descending on the earth
And tearing firm mountains from their roots.
Those who know say even its lungs spit fire
Whose great flames shatter the earth
So that in the minds of all
It symbolised the wrath of the gods.

In all this the power of the creator
Revealed itself in his daughter, the princess of life, Nomkhubul-
   wane.
She was the source of all life.
She gave abundance to the hungry of the earth.
For this even animals hailed her in their worlds
And gambolled like young calves at play.
The princess of life was loved for her songs,
Whoever heard them would lie down
Repeating their music over and over again in his heart.
Even on this day of august debates
They all listened as she touched on the unknown and beautiful
   themes,
Saying: 'We have fulfilled the other tasks of creation
But they are not complete without man,
He who will bind all things of existence,
A great shepherd who excels with wisdom.'
She did not indulge in long endless debates
Since even those who listened to her took long to understand
As on the day of creation they did not understand.
But Somazwi dreaded by all, who speaks with the vehemence of
   fire
Did not wait long, like all who are poised with suspicion
Terrified of the power that challenges them in their glory,
They who follow all new ideas with the violence of their eyes.
He replied like one whose words burn the lips
And said: 'Here begins again the old tale of blunders
As when long ago we remonstrated in the wind
Saying it is enough that our great assembly exists,
We, the ultimate expression of the power of the creator.
But now we hear this strange story of a new power
That will supervise all things with knowledge.'
He spoke as they all listened with extended ears
Knowing that though they did not hold affection for him
His mind was as swift as the horn of a bull.

His followers clustered together like a brood,
As always, applauding each word he put forward.
Others delighted in the clash of words
Saying let the giants show their strength.
They waited for Sodume,
Whose intelligence baffled those known for their wisdom
As if even the winds listened when he spoke.
Somazwi continued: 'What will this creature
Do with knowledge that excels all created things
Endowed as they are with enough for each day.
On the next day they still have enough for their daily needs
But I fear that this creature on knowing so much
Will experience the pains of yesterday and the unfulfilled to-
    morrow.
When it realises the defects of its clan
It will build dreams that will never be fulfilled
And wander everywhere with painful doubts asking the question
"What is the earth, of what value is life?"
It will not be enough to revel in the beauties of an earthly life.'
He spoke so wisely that even those who supported Nomkhubul-
    wane
Began to doubt and were swayed by Somazwi's thoughts.
All shook in their seats with questions.
Sodume alone listened
As if inspired by visions others could not reach.
He turned to his wife who rested her hand on his shoulder
Saying: 'The life we live deprives us of wisdom,
We are overwhelmed by things before us.'
Scarcely had he finished these words when someone stood
Turning to him as if he heard him:
'Great fighter who overwhelms with fierce powers
Do not allow the fire of words to burn beautiful things
As if these words were the very kernel of truth.
Unsheath your thoughts and cut these poisonous doubts
Of even those who have been swayed.

92

We all know a great path leads forward.
In it, all solutions evolve.
You, with only a few words, can straighten crooked thoughts.'
He was silent and so were all the others.
It was as if whoever spoke first would create great conflagrations.
Sodume did not respond.
He listened like all wise men
Who do not rush without untying each knot.
Sometimes when they discover the truth they only laugh in their
    hearts
Knowing how words are like seeds
Which fall from the hands in their hundreds, most dying in their
    shells.
One who was known for his love of pleasure stood up
And thought he might speak.
So that they may remember pots frothing with beer
He said: 'How can we solve in a day such great mysteries
We must settle down under the shade delving into the truth.'
Others stared at each other pleased with these words
But none was eager to be seen filled with enthusiasm
Since there must be no talk of hunger in great assemblies.
Opponents continued to talk fiercely
Saying: 'The creation of man is no desire of the creator'
It seemed those who opposed the creation of man would triumph
Bidding with their words saying:
'This foolish creature will walk blindly, knowing and yet not
    knowing.
Since a pleasant life must define its boundaries.'

After a long debate
Nomkhubulwane was heard asking for their attention.
She called over and over again as she had provoked the debate.
As she stood up the sun shook with her shadow
Addressing him who favoured beasts to man,
She said: 'These arguments of the day have strange forebodings.

Those who oppose the hand of creation
Do so believing that what is, is complete.
But they do not understand, creation must always create.
Its essence is its change.
From it abundance splits itself to make abundance.
Whoever loves its greatness does not question it
Since to question is to weave strange tangles.
Its greatness is its expanse as always.
Somazwi and all those who are swept by his words do not know
That this creature, man, shall derive his power
From the very struggle of incomplete power
Which alone will rouse his mind with the appetite for wisdom.'
She spoke these words knowing what lay hidden in their fears.
Even now the truth of what was to come formed itself within
    them.
They all listened, even the excitable followers of Somazwi
Since they still held her high in their esteem not for prestige,
But for her thoughts that burn like a thin sword.
He who had long depended on wisdom for his fame called out.
As he began to talk they all turned their eyes
Guessing what wisdom Sodume was to unravel.
'I have listened to the skilful tongues
Saying what value will it be to man
That he should walk in ignorance, blind of his fate.
But such questions and remarks have their weaknesses.
Whoever is the umbilical cord of life denies his existence
If he disputes the oneness of which he is extension.
It is not he alone who is, who is the reality of creation,
But those who are and others who shall be
Since the eye of life extends to the vastness of eternity.
The daughter of heaven has spoken all truths.
Whoever has not heard
Harbours his own kind of truth which he shall not reveal before
    us.'
The great gathering listened,

94

Each trying to untie the profound meanings in Sodume's words.
Others questioned these thoughts saying truth is always relative
But others could not reach conclusions,
Their faces rigid with amazement.
Sodume continued: 'The mind is the essence of conquest.
If man is endowed with this power
Even lions who boast their strength will fear him.
I and others who love the extension of life
Say let men stand supreme over the earth.'

The chorus of those who agreed echoed
And as was customary a great anthem was heard
A eulogy from those who favoured mankind.
Someone from the assembly shouted:
'It is ours, this voice, it is ours.'
When this mysterious debate was over, they all dispersed in their
    ways.
There were great feasts at the house of Somahle
Who was the source of all pleasure;
Whoever entered this house revelled as he wished.
A great hubbub was heard as they laughed and drank.
Some held beer pots decorated with stars
Some mocked others saying: 'You were silent, great talker'
Addressing him who never spoke but always listened.
Sodume threw a ball of fire
Displaying flashes of lightning in the distant horizon
Its flashes making paths in the sky
Those who like to play sped down on them
Swinging from ray to ray as they descended to the earth.